W9-AGZ-841

AWESOME VALUES IN FAMOUS LIVES

Gloria Estefan

Never Give Up

Barbara Kramer

Enslow Elementary
an imprint of

Enslow Publishers, Inc.

40 Industrial Road	PO Box 38
Box 398	Aldershot
Berkeley Heights, NJ 07922	Hants GU12 6BP
USA	UK

http://www.enslow.com

Enslow Elementary, an imprint of Enslow Publishers, Inc.

Enslow Elementary® is a registered trademark of Enslow Publishers, Inc.

Copyright © 2005 by Enslow Publishers, Inc.

All rights reserved.

No part of this book may be reproduced by any means without the written permission of the publisher.

Library of Congress Cataloging-in-Publication Data

Kramer, Barbara.
   Gloria Estefan : never give up / Barbara Kramer.
      p. cm.— (Awesome values in famous lives)
   Includes bibliographical references (p.) and index.
   ISBN 0-7660-2380-X (hardcover)
   1. Estefan, Gloria—Juvenile literature.
2. Singers—United States—Biography—Juvenile literature. I. Title. II. Series.
ML3930.E85K73 2004
782.42164'092—dc22

                                              2004004502

Printed in the United States of America

10 9 8 7 6 5 4 3 2 1

To Our Readers: We have done our best to make sure all Internet Addresses in this book were active and appropriate when we went to press. However, the author and the publisher have no control over and assume no liability for the material available on those Internet sites or on other Web sites they may link to. Any comments or suggestions can be sent by e-mail to comments@enslow.com or to the address on the back cover.

Every effort has been made to locate all copyright holders of material used in this book. If any errors or omissions have occurred, corrections will be made in future editions of this book.

Illustration Credits: AP/Wide World, pp. 4–5, 8L, 17, 19, 23L, 26, 27, 29, 30, 32, 34, 36-37, 38, 39, 41, 43L, 43R; Artville LLC, pp. 7, 20R; Classmates.com, pp. 12–13C, 13R; Estefan Enterprises, pp. 6, 11, 15; Hemera Technologies Inc., pp. 2, 9R, 10, 18, 20L, 23R, 31; Historical Association of Southern Florida, Miami News Collection, pp. 8–9C; Miami Herald, p. 16; photos.com, p. 24; Private Collection, p. 22; Raul Demolina/Shooting Star, p. 25.

Cover Illustration: AP/Wide World

Contents

Gloria Estefan
is often called
the "Queen
of Latin Pop."

"One Day You're Going to Be a Great Star"

O nstage, in the spotlight, Gloria Estefan is having fun. She sings and dances in a whirl of excitement. "The rhythm is gonna get you!" Gloria's energy zips through the crowd. Thousands of fans jump to their feet— clapping, cheering, singing, dancing.

Gloria's family called her "Glorita."
That is Spanish for "little Gloria."

It is hard to believe that Gloria was once a shy, lonely child. That is just one of many challenges she has faced on her road to success. But Gloria says problems are just part of life.[1] Those hard times have made her strong.

Gloria Marie Fajardo was born on September 1, 1957, in Havana, on the island of Cuba. Her father, José Fajardo, worked as a bodyguard for the family of Cuba's president, Fulgencio Batista. Her mother, also named Gloria, was a teacher.

In 1959, rebel soldiers took over the government of Cuba. Fidel Castro became the new leader. Gloria's father knew that Castro would punish anyone who had worked for Batista. Like many other Cubans, José and his family fled the island. Gloria was sixteen months old. Her family went first to Texas and then settled in Miami, Florida.

Gloria was born in Cuba and moved to the United States.

The government of the United States did not like Castro's government. In 1961, the United States made a secret plan. They trained about 1,300 Cuban Americans to help. José Fajardo and the other men were sent into Cuba to fight to overthrow Castro.

The plan did not work. Gloria's father and more than 1,000 other men were captured and put into a Cuban prison.

Gloria and her mother were left on their own in the city of Miami. They lived in a tiny apartment and had

When Fidel Castro became the leader of Cuba, Gloria's family had to leave the country.

So many Cubans moved to Miami that one part of the city was called "Little Havana."

very little money. At first, they used newspapers as the sheets on their beds. They made their food in tin cans because they had no pots.

The neighbors all pooled their money to buy an old car for $50. Only one woman knew how to drive. She drove everyone else to the grocery store to buy food.[2]

Gloria missed her father. Her mother said he was "on the farm,"

Little Havana

In Little Havana, the people spoke Spanish. They listened to Cuban music and cooked Cuban foods. But some people in Miami did not like anyone who was different. They treated Cubans badly. At some apartment buildings, signs were posted: NO CHILDREN. NO PETS. NO CUBANS. This was not right, and it was hurtful to Gloria and the other Cubans.

but Gloria knew the truth. On her fifth birthday, she was sad because her father was still in jail.[3] A few months later, just before Christmas, he came home.

Gloria's father joined the United States Army, and the family had to move to an army base in Texas. There, Gloria started going to school. She liked learning English, and she even won an award for being a good reader. Gloria's sister, Rebecca, was born in Texas.

When Gloria was nine, her father was sent to fight in a war in the country of Vietnam. Gloria's mother took the girls back to live in Miami. She had always loved music, and she bought Gloria a guitar. It turned out to be a very special gift. Gloria liked to play her guitar along with the songs on the radio.

Gloria sang along with popular music on the radio.

Playing the guitar helped when Gloria felt sad.

Sometimes she taped her songs and mailed them to her father. Proudly, he played them for the other soldiers. Then he wrote to Gloria: "One day you're going to be a great star."[4]

❝Music was the
one bright spot
in my life.**❞**[5]

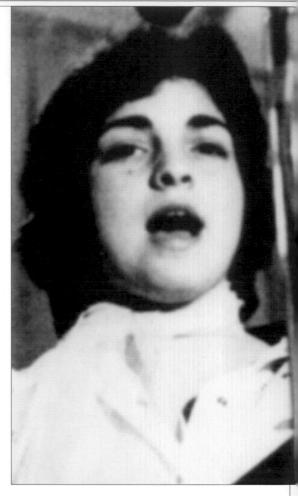

In 1968, when Gloria
was ten, her father came
home from the war in
Vietnam. Soon after, he
became very sick. Doctors
said that he had multiple
sclerosis (called MS). The
disease made his muscles
weak, and he fell down a lot. Sometimes he got all
mixed up. He did things like stopping his car for a
green light when he was supposed to go.

Gloria's mother worked in the daytime. At night,
she took classes so she could be a teacher in the

In high school, Gloria played her guitar and sang in talent shows.

United States. Gloria was left in charge of her father and her sister.

After school every day, Gloria had work to do. Her father needed to be fed and washed.

For Gloria, music was her escape. "I would just sit in my room for hours and hours and write songs and poetry," she said.[6]

By the time Gloria was sixteen, her father was too sick to live at home anymore. Gloria went to see him every day in the hospital. It was a sad time for the family, and Gloria filled the lonely hours with her music.

Gloria earned top grades at the all-girls high school she attended.

CHAPTER 2

Miami Sound Machine

loria graduated from high school in 1975. That summer, she and some friends put together a band just for fun. A local boy, Emilio Estefan, stopped by one day to give them a few tips. He was the leader of a band called the Miami Latin Boys.

Gloria saw Emilio again a few months later. The Miami Latin Boys were playing at a wedding, and Gloria was one of the guests. Emilio remembered Gloria—and her great voice. Would she sing a few numbers with the band? At first Gloria said no, but Emilio talked her into performing.

Gloria had never taken any singing lessons, but she was a hit with the wedding guests. Later, Emilio invited Gloria to join his band. She agreed to sing with them on weekends.

During the week, Gloria was a student at the University of Miami. She earned A's in almost all her classes. She took a French class, and soon her skill in speaking three languages—Spanish, English, and French—paid off. Gloria took a

Gloria studied psychology in college. Psychology is the science of the mind and how people think and act.

When Gloria first joined Miami Sound Machine,
everyone took turns as the singer.

part-time job as an interpreter at Miami International
Airport. She helped people who did not speak English.

After Gloria joined the band, the Miami Latin
Boys changed their name to Miami Sound Machine
(MSM). They played Latin music with Spanish lyrics

and a strong dance beat. They also played some of the latest hit songs from the radio. Miami Sound Machine grew very popular. They played at special events like weddings and *quinces*. These are big parties for Latin girls turning fifteen.

Miami Sound Machine had no lead singer. The band members took turns. At first, Gloria was glad to sing backup. "I didn't want to be in the spotlight," she said.[1] But she was changing. Performing onstage was helping Gloria overcome her shyness.

In the spring of 1978, Gloria graduated from college with top honors. She had studied psychology, but now she wanted to focus on her music. How far would it take her?

Emilio was Gloria's first boyfriend. They began dating about a year after Gloria joined the band.

Shy Gloria

Gloria wanted to sing her best and look her best. She did not want to feel so shy onstage. Gloria looked at videotapes of Miami Sound Machine. What could she do differently? As she worked hard to improve herself, she started feeling more confident.

Gloria's interest in music had also brought love into her life. On September 2, 1978, she married Emilio Estefan. Gloria was twenty-one; Emilio was twenty-five. That same year, Miami Sound Machine came out with its first album. Some songs were in Spanish; some were in English. In the next two years, the band made two more albums with both Spanish and English songs.

Gloria's father died in 1980, but there was also happiness that year when her son, Nayib, was born. For the band, there was good news, too. They would record four albums for the Latin-music branch of CBS Records.

Gloria and MSM won the grand prize at this 1986 music festival in Tokyo, Japan.

The record company wanted all the songs to be in Spanish because the band was so popular in Spanish-speaking countries. At MSM's concerts in Central and South America, fans packed the stadiums.

Danger Tour

Touring can be full of surprises. One time, the band was in the war-torn country of El Salvador in Central America. To protect the band, armed guards stood ready with machine guns. When Miami Sound Machine came onstage, there were loud cracks, like gunfire. "We all hit the deck," said Gloria.[2] A few minutes later, they learned the reason for the noise: fireworks to welcome the band. Gloria and MSM felt a bit embarrassed, but "the audience just laughed," she said.[3]

But in the United States, hardly anyone outside the city of Miami had even heard of them. That was something Gloria wanted to change.[4] She and Emilio wanted to make Latin music popular all over America.

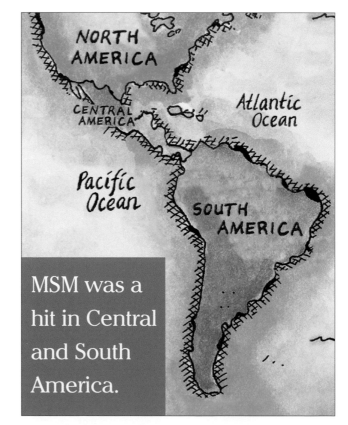

MSM was a hit in Central and South America.

CHAPTER 3

"Dr. Beat" and the Conga

Miami Sound Machine had a lively new dance song, "Dr. Beat." Would CBS let the band record it in English? The record company agreed to put "Dr. Beat" on the B side of a single. The A side would be a Spanish song.[1]

One day, a radio station in Miami played "Dr. Beat." Listeners started calling. They wanted to

The B Side

Each single record had two sides. Side 1, also called the A side, held the song predicted to be a hit—and that was what radio stations usually played. The song on Side 2, or the B side, was not played as much.

hear the song again and again. "Dr. Beat" became one of the most popular songs on the radio station. Soon, it became a hit across the United States and Europe.

The success of "Dr. Beat" showed CBS that English-speaking people liked Miami Sound Machine, too. The band began to work with Epic Records, the rock-music branch of CBS.[2] Miami Sound Machine was not just for Latin listeners anymore.

In 1984, Miami Sound Machine made its first album in English, *Eyes of Innocence*. One of the songs on the album was "Dr. Beat." By then, Gloria was the band's lead singer. She was also writing some of the songs. Two of them were recorded on *Eyes of Innocence*.

The album did well in Europe, but it was not as popular in the United States. MSM enjoyed more success with *Primitive Love* (1985). To promote this new album, Miami Sound Machine

The conga is usually danced in a single-file line. Dancers place their hands on the hips of the person in front of them. Then they zigzag about the room. The dance pattern is Step-step-step, kick! Step-step-step, kick!

Gloria leads a conga line in New York City.

Crossover Music

Pop, jazz, classical, country, Latin . . . These are just a few of the many different styles of music. Gloria is special because she is a crossover musician. That means her music is popular with fans of more than one musical style. "Conga" was the first song in recording history to be a hit with fans of four different styles of music—dance, pop, Latin, and R&B/Hip-Hop.

went on tour. The band played more than one hundred concerts in the United States, Central America, Europe, and Asia. The song "Conga" became MSM's first big English-language hit.

MSM ended all its concerts with "Conga," and many cities held contests for the longest conga line. Miami won when 119,984 people formed a conga line that stretched almost three miles.[3]

In 1987 MSM released its next album, *Let It Loose*. Emilio no longer played in the band. Instead, he was Miami Sound Machine's manager. He also produced records for other singers.

Emilio and Nayib did not go on the *Let It Loose* tour with the band. For the first time in many years,

Gloria was on her own.[4] Between concerts, Gloria wrote new songs and worked out. She needed to be strong and fit for her high-energy dancing onstage. She trained like an athlete, with four-mile runs and as many as 600 sit-ups.[5]

Gloria's trainer helped her stay in shape for her concerts.

By 1989, Gloria was featured as a solo act, with MSM playing backup.

The *Let It Loose* album was a big success. Miami Sound Machine won an American Music Award for best pop rock group of the year. After the tour, Gloria took time off to relax in the dream house that she and Emilio had built on Star Island, off the coast of Florida.

For Miami Sound Machine, times were changing.

Their next album, *Cuts Both Ways*, was released in 1989. By then, all the musicians from the Miami Latin Boys had left the group. Other musicians played guitar and drums, and Gloria was the singer. Now Miami Sound Machine was a backup band for Gloria's solo act.

In the spring of 1989, Broadcast Music Inc. gave Gloria an award as Songwriter of the Year. She was the first Latin woman to receive this honor.[6] In the fall, she headed for Europe to begin a new world tour.

Gloria accepted the American Music Award for Miami Sound Machine on January 30, 1989.

"I'm Cuban American....I have an American head and a Cuban heart."[7]

CHAPTER 4

Gloria's Biggest Challenge

O n her *Cuts Both Ways* tour, Gloria played to packed crowds in England, Scotland, Holland, and Belgium. Next came concerts in cities across the United States.

Even when she was sick with the flu, Gloria kept on performing. Then she got a bad sore throat and began to worry. Throat problems can ruin a singer's career.

"I was really scared," she said. Singing "is my life."[1] A doctor told Gloria that she must not sing at all for two months. So she canceled her concerts and went home to Miami.

By March 1990, Gloria was back on the road, playing the concerts she had missed. But her troubles were not over. On March 20, the Miami Sound Machine tour bus was caught in a raging snowstorm in Pennsylvania.

On the bus with Gloria were Emilio, Nayib, Nayib's teacher, and Gloria's assistant.

Gloria's tour bus was in a terrible accident.

Gloria was napping when the bus stopped moving. An accident blocked the road ahead.

Suddenly, a speeding truck rammed into the back of the bus. Gloria was hurled to the floor. The bus crashed again as it slammed forward into a truck.

Nayib and Emilio seemed okay. But Gloria did not move. Horrible pain ripped through her back.

Outside, the roads were slick with ice. An hour passed before an ambulance could reach the bus.

At the hospital, the X-rays showed what Gloria had already feared. Her back was broken. Nayib had a broken collarbone, but it would easily heal. The others had only minor injuries.

The next day, Gloria was flown to a hospital in New York City for a four-hour operation. The surgeon put two eight-inch metal rods in her back. One rod was on each side of her spine. It took four hundred stitches to sew her up.

As soon as Gloria's fans heard about the accident, thousands of cards, letters, and flowers came pouring in. She received 4,000 flower arrangements and more than 48,000 cards.

Two weeks later, Gloria flew home to Miami on a friend's private jet. At first, she could not do everyday tasks like bathing and dressing herself. Gloria did not like being helpless. After her father became so sick, she had lived with a secret fear that something would happen to her.[2]

Nayib greets his mom as she arrives back in Miami after her surgery.

Constant pain made sleeping hard, too. But Gloria was a fighter. She began to do some exercises in the swimming pool and on an exercise bike. It was not easy. There were plenty of days when she wanted to skip the exercises. But Gloria did not give in to those feelings. "I've always been a person who believes if there's something to be done, you do it. That's what helped me through," she said later.[3]

Getting back to her music was hard, too. Three months after the accident, Gloria still did not feel like singing or writing songs. One day, Emilio called her into the music room. A few words had popped into his head when Gloria was on her way to the hospital in New York City: "Coming out of the dark."[4]

Ideas began to swirl through Gloria's mind, and she started to write. "Coming Out of the Dark" was one of thirteen new songs for her next album, *Into the Light* (1991).

"Step by step, I'll make it through," sang Gloria in "Into the Light."[5]

Gloria's first time back onstage was at the American Music Awards show, January 28, 1991. "My heart started beating so hard, I thought it was going to come out of my chest," she said.[6] Then she started to sing, and everything felt right.

In March 1991, almost a year after the accident, Gloria set out on a world tour for *Into the Light*. She was in better shape than ever. "I just have to make sure I don't do crazy things, like backflips off the stage," she joked.[7]

Gloria returned to the concert stage in triumph for her *Into the Light* tour.

CHAPTER 5

"Reach"

In August 1992, Hurricane Andrew battered southern Florida, causing billions of dollars of damage. The Estefans' house survived the violent winds, but Gloria's heart reached out to the thousands of people whose homes were destroyed.

Gloria and Emilio put together a concert that raised about $3 million to help victims of the hurricane. Then Gloria recorded a new song, "Always Tomorrow." It told people not to give up—to look ahead to better days. Gloria gave all the money from sales of the song to a hurricane relief fund.

Hurricane Andrew destroyed more than 25,000 homes.

In 1993, Gloria released a new album, *Mi Tierra* (My Homeland), with some of the Cuban songs that her grandmother had sung. Gloria had also written new songs in the musical style of her Cuban roots. She knew she was taking a risk. Would her English-speaking fans like an album of Spanish songs?

The answer was clear when *Mi Tierra* sold 5 million copies around the world. It also won a

Grammy Award for the Best Tropical Latin Album.

On Gloria's next album, *Hold Me, Thrill Me, Kiss Me*, all the songs were in English. It was released in October 1994, two months before her daughter, Emily, was born.

In 1995, another Spanish-language album, *Abriendo Puertas* (Opening Doors), earned Gloria a Grammy for Best Tropical Latin Performance. Then, in 1996, a song on her new album *Destiny* brought Gloria a different kind of honor. "Reach" is about being strong and trying to do your best. It was the theme song for the Summer Olympic Games in Atlanta, Georgia.

After singing "Reach" at the closing ceremony of

Gloria's voice rang out at the Olympics.

the Olympics, Gloria launched into "Conga." To her surprise, the Olympic athletes made a conga line and began to step, kick, and dance. For Gloria, it was a thrilling moment.

All her life, Gloria has been known as a helpful, caring person. As a celebrity, she has continued to give her time and money to help others. In 1997, she started the Gloria Estefan Foundation to raise money for research for cancer, AIDS, and spinal cord injuries.

In 1998, for a new challenge, Gloria took a small part in a movie, *Music of My Heart*. The movie's theme song, which Gloria recorded with the group 'N Sync, quickly became a hit.

Acting was fun, but music is still the heart of Gloria's career. In 2001, she and Emilio were honored with a place in the Songwriters Hall of Fame.

Gloria, Emilio, Nayib, and Emily in 2001.

Gloria's next album, *Unwrapped* (2003), was very personal. Every song was like a snapshot of an event in Gloria's life. "To every memory in my head, there's music attached to it," she said.[1] Gloria's twenty-three-year-old son, Nayib, made a DVD to go with the album. *Famous* shows Gloria at home with her family.

Gloria Estefan has sold more than 70 million albums. Unlike many other Latin singers, she never chose between Latin music and pop music. Instead, she sings both, and her crossover success has brought together fans from two cultures. Gloria has won awards for her singing and for her work to help other people. Facing her life's challenges helped Gloria find the power inside herself. "She is a tower of strength," said one friend. "She looks little, but she's a giant inside."[2]

"You've got to believe," says Gloria. "Never be afraid to dream."[3]

Timeline

1957	Born on September 1, in Havana, Cuba.
1960	Settles in Miami, Florida, with her parents.
1975	Graduates from high school; joins Miami Sound Machine.
1978	Graduates from the University of Miami; marries Emilio Estefan.
1980	Son, Nayib, is born.
1984	Records *Eyes of Innocence*, Miami Sound Machine's first English-language album.
1989	Gloria is featured as a single artist on *Cuts Both Ways*; receives award as Songwriter of the Year from Broadcast Music Inc.
1990	Gloria's back is broken in bus accident.
1994	Daughter, Emily, is born.
2001	Is inducted into the Songwriters Hall of Fame.
2003	Releases *Unwrapped*, an album about her life.

Music by Gloria Estefan
A SELECTED LIST

Eyes of Innocence, 1984

Primitive Love, 1985

Let It Loose, 1987

Cuts Both Ways, 1989

Into the Light, 1991

Greatest Hits, 1992

Mi Tierra, 1993

Christmas Through Your Eyes, 1993

Hold Me, Thrill Me, Kiss Me, 1994

Abriendo Puertas, 1995

Destiny, 1996

gloria!, 1998

Alma Caribena, 2000

Greatest Hits Vol. II, 2001

Unwrapped, 2003

Words to Know

backup band—A band that plays music to accompany a singer.

Grammy—An award for excellence in the music business.

interpreter—Someone who can understand words in one language and then say the same thing in a different language.

lyrics—The words to a song.

manager—A boss; a person in charge of a business.

promote—To create interest in a product or an idea.

rebel—Fighting against a ruler or the government.

tour—To travel from city to city. A singer goes on tour to give concerts.

Chapter Notes

CHAPTER 1.
"One Day You're Going to Be a Great Star"

1. Peter Castro, "Little Glorita, Happy at Last," *People*, August 12, 1996, p. 62.

2. Leonard Pitts, Jr., "Miami's Patron Saint," *Entertainment Weekly*, July 30, 1993, p. 55(1).

3. *Biography Today*, July 1992, p. 54.

4. Christopher John Farley, "From a Cuban Heart," *Time*, July 8, 1996, p. 68.

5. "Ole! Gloria Estefan," *New York Times Magazine*, October 23, 1994, p. 35.

6. Sheryl Berk, "Livin' la Vida Gloria," *McCall's*, November 1999, p. 53.

CHAPTER 2.
Miami Sound Machine

1. Richard Harrington, "Miami Voice: How Shy, Cuban-Born Gloria Estefan Came to Power the Sound Machine," *Washington Post*, July 17, 1988, p. G1.

2. (sidebar) John Milward, "Gloria Estefan: Living in Two Worlds," *TV Guide*, January 20, 1990, p. 20.

3. (sidebar) Milward, p. 21.

4. Grace Catalano, *Gloria Estefan* (New York: St. Martin's Press, 1991), p. 62.

CHAPTER 3.
"Dr. Beat" and the Conga

1. Grace Catalano, *Gloria Estefan* (New York: St. Martin's Press, 1991), p. 66.

2. "Gloria Estefan," *Current Biography*, October 1995, p. 21.

3. Anthony M. DeStefano, *Gloria Estefan: The Pop Superstar from Tragedy to Triumph* (New York: Penguin Putnam, Inc., 1997), p. 44.

4. Catalano, p. 100.

5. Juan Carlos Coto, "Gloria Estefan Fights to Make a Crucial Comeback," *San Jose Mercury News*, July 4, 1990, p. 1D.

Chapter Notes

6. Jim Bessman, "Gloria's Songwriting Has a Global Reach," *Billboard*, October 11, 2003, p. 34.

7. Christopher John Farley, "From a Cuban Heart," *Time*, July 8, 1996, p. 68.

CHAPTER 4.
Gloria's Biggest Challenge

1. Daisann McLane, "The Power & the Gloria," *Rolling Stone*, June 14, 1990, p. 74.

2. Gloria Estefan and Kathryn Casey, "My Miracle," *Ladies' Home Journal*, August 1990, p. 152.

3. Ileane Rudolph, "Power & Gloria," *TV Guide*, January 23, 1993, p. 20.

4. Steve Dougherty, "A Year After Her Brush with Disaster, Gloria Estefan Dances Out of the Dark with a New Album and World Tour," *People*, February 18, 1991, p. 118.

5. Patrick MacDonald, "G-L-O-R-I-A: If the Grit and Strength Don't Get You, the Rhythm Will," *Seattle Times*, August 2, 1991, Tempo section, p. 3.

6. Dougherty, p. 118.

7. Susan Korones Gifford, "Red Hot Right Now," *Cosmopolitan*, June 1991, p. 108.

CHAPTER 5.
"Reach"

1. *Famous* DVD, written, produced, and directed by Nayib Estefan. Packaged and released with Gloria's CD *Unwrapped*, Sony Music Entertainment, 2003.

2. Quote from Cristina Saralegui in Quincy Jones, et. al., "A Star in Every Sense of the Word," *Billboard*, October 11, 2003, pp. 42+.

3. From "Nayib's Song (I Am Here for You)."

Learn More

Books

Benson, Michael. *Gloria Estefan*. Minneapolis: Lerner Publishing Group, 2000.

Boulais, Sue. *Gloria Estefan*. Bear, Del.: Mitchell Lane Publishers, Inc., 1998.

Gonzalez, Fernando. *Gloria Estefan: Cuban-American Singing Star*. Brookfield, Conn.: Millbrook Press, 1993.

Rodriguez, Janel. *Gloria Estefan*. New York: Raintree/Steck Vaughn Publishers, 1995.

Strazzabosco, Jeanne M. *Learning About Determination From the Life of Gloria Estefan*. New York: PowerKids Press, 1997.

Internet Addresses

Gloria's official website includes photos, videos, music, and a place to send email messages to her.
    <http://www.gloriaestefan.com>

Brief information about Gloria's background, her successes, and her music.
    <http://www.musicfaves.com/estefan>

Index

Pages with photographs are in **boldface** type.